The Diary of an Inspirational

Harvey took over our lives as soon as he arrived. There was no transition period and there were no conscious tactics on our part. He came to us temporarily while our daughter-in-law was ill and here he stayed fitting himself into our retirement like a comfortable old slipper.

We laid down no rules and although we allowed him the freedom of the house from the start he decided firmly on what would be his own lifestyle, limitations and place in the family set up. His chosen base under the kitchen table is the hub of the house where he keeps a close watch on comings and goings. He regulates his life from there.

Harvey has always been his own man and we wouldn't have him any way other than the one he has prescribed for himself.

To us he is a philosophical fur ball with attitude whose diary is a true reflection of the life he leads ... but let him tell you himself.

Janet Toseland

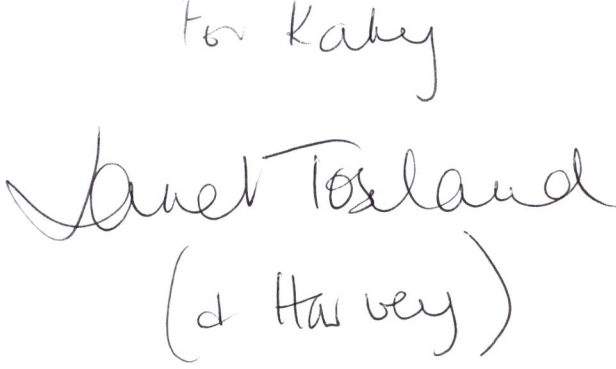

For Celia, Twigs and house rabbits everywhere

© Janet Toseland 2012

All rights reserved. No part of this publication may be reproduced or transmitted in any way or by any means without permission in writing.

Published by Figaro Publishing

ISBN 978-0-9573754-0-6

Designed by John Williams
Printed by Cambridge Digital Press

Introducing me

I am Harvey. Janet is my primary care giver. She lives with me and I train her. I am a black, nine year old mini lop-eared house rabbit. Welcome to my life.

As far as I can remember, living with people began the day I was bought for thirty pounds from a pet shop at a few weeks old and was mostly a big fluffy head with floppy ears. I suppose I might have been a bit bossy even then. My dog Willow, in my first house soon got used to being told where she was allowed to sit and when she could play with me. My game rules of course. We were great buddies. It's nice to look at old photographs and reminisce especially on a cold winter day but this was all before I came to live in my new home with the older generation when my real work began.

It's not all cabbage and carrots being in charge of two humans and a house. Every day brings something new. Fresh training sessions for my family, having to sort through stuff left lying around, finding different ways of making my bed, trimming the herbs by the back door, testing new food, welcoming visitors and keeping track of life in general. There's always something interesting going on so I thought the best thing to do was start a diary to show just how much work I do to keep everything running smoothly and to prove what a great asset I am to the family.

January

A new beginning

I've decided not to make any resolutions this year. There isn't much I want to change. My food is good apart from carrots being thin on the ground. The green tops make up for it a bit but they're not as sweet and crunchy as the other end. No, on the whole I'm very comfortable and happy and still have plenty of spare time to think and plan and keep my household organised to rabbit standards.

I was going to resolve to make more fuss at wash and brush up time every morning but it wouldn't make any difference, it would still happen. I know I feel fresh and ready for the day when it's over but really hate the idea of it. It's only at one end after all and warm water isn't so bad so it's best to just close my eyes and think of dandelions. I'm pretty perfect in every other way though.

In trouble

It hasn't been a good start to the year. I flicked the lid from a dish someone had put on my window seat look-out and accidentally chipped a bit off. I only wanted to look inside in case some carrot had been hidden there. They are always hiding tasty things in different places for me to find in case I get bored. How was I to know it was a special, hundred year old tureen? Who wants something that old anyway? What's the use of having a dish in the kitchen if there is no food in it? It seems pointless to me.

The plumber came later and while I was lending him a paw I found the humane mouse trap behind a cupboard so I wrecked that by tossing it about on the tiles. I could smell some delicious cereal inside and why should a mouse have it instead of me? It was on the floor, my floor so it should have been mine. Anyway, it's broken now so I'm going to forget about it. It's all the fault of the family for teaching me to hunt for food. I tried to make up for it by helping the plumber to look for plums but couldn't find any. A bit of ripe plum can be very tasty.

January

Let it Snow

There's nothing like fresh, healthy greens to brighten a winter day. My stocks should last until the snow clears. The utility room is out of bounds because they think the quarry tiles are too cold for my feet. Personally I think they are being over protective so I keep a wary eye on the door and sneak out to cool down when they're not looking. In the meantime I'm being coddled like an egg. My feet have fur on them for goodness sake and some rabbits are still living in hutches in freezing gardens. Why is this? Why can't they come indoors and share a fire with their families? I don't mind popping outside for a few minutes when they feed the birds because I need to keep a check on how many of my raisins go onto their feeding patch but never stay there for very long. I feel sorry for the birds. A big brown Labrador came into the garden today and ate their two cheese and raisin scones with extra fat, some grated cheese, chopped apple and a scoop of mealworm crumble. I expect it was sick when it got home.

Cut and blow dry

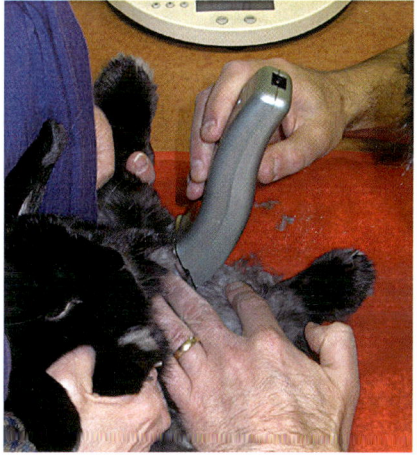

There's one good thing about going to the vet, you realise you are not the only one with problems. Mine was the usual rear end shave this time. It took ages because they chatted with my doctor about all kinds of unnecessary stuff instead of letting him get on with the job. I lay there in a most ungainly and unmanly position while they discussed new web sites and how to take a cat's blood pressure instead of concentrating on me. My skin around that area is tissue paper thin and needs very careful handling.

I was very impressed with Chloe the cat who was in the waiting room with me. She made a huge fuss and palaver in her carrying cage, shredding her newspaper bedding to let everybody know how much she objected to being there. She is nearly nineteen so she is very experienced at showing her displeasure. Her human mum just smiled and said, "She always does this when she comes here." Of course she does. How else can she explain she isn't happy and wants to go home? I'm going to practice my shredding technique today.

January

Ways and Means

I've been working on a couple of new methods of getting behind the television when cushions have been stuffed down each side. With a bit of scrabbling it's easy to pull them out then climb over if my family is dozing which happens often these days. You need to keep planning when you are a house rabbit. After all, in the wild there would be new burrows to design all the time so a regular inspection into the dark hole behind the TV set is good practice. If they're wide awake and watching me, this is what I've tried and it works pretty well. First of all I dash round the room flipping the occasional binky to entertain them then without pausing for a second I dive mid-flight behind the television set before they realise what has happened. This brings loud hand clapping, shouts of, "Harvey, Harvey" and other screams of delight. They love it.

Then there's my gangster method. I mooch nonchalantly backwards and forwards in front of the screen looking casually in another direction as if I'm casing the joint then suddenly twist and jump with expert precision down the side of the set. They never expect it. I love a good chuckle. People don't realise what a sense of humour we have unless they keep rabbits themselves. I planned all this to get my own back on J, my primary care giver who started hiding behind the sofa at playtime. She surprised me a couple of times but after that I expected it and crept along behind her. I was so quiet she didn't know where I was so she was the one who got the surprise. We often play together on the floor.

January

Refresher Course

It's definitely time for a refresher course for the family. Nobody is up to scratch and they are getting lax and lazy. For instance, if I sit on my back legs in my basket I should get carrot. If I sit on the corner of the kitchen mat I should be given a nibble or two of apple and pear. Surely that is easy enough for anybody to understand. If I sit at J's feet and look up I need my head and ears stroked so I can push my face between her fingers and give her a good wash. When I stare at a closed door it means I want it opened. If I turn my back I want to be left alone to think. Is that easy or not?

Any human two year old could learn these things considering the number of times a day I run through them but until she learns my silent language there is no point in moving on to the latest instruction which is to leave me upstairs to play in my burrows for as long as I like.

Then there are my important stamping rules. One stamp means, "Here I am, I'm in the room, watch me please." Or "I'm behind the television, so there!" Or "Don't you dare poop-check me."

Could I make things any easier for her? As a house rabbit there's no need to thump for danger the way I would do in the wild so I might as well use this rabbit know-how for training purposes.

February

A handsome chap

All my jobs were finished by eight-o-clock this morning. I'd punched the end flap down in my cardboard tunnel, eaten my morning bit of carrot, dashed upstairs to check on M, my second in command, cleaned J's hand and tried to pull her bed socks off with my teeth. After a thorough face wash there was nothing else to do but sit it out until breakfast time. Then I spotted this on the floor ready to throw away. It was a bit of a surprise to start with but when I peered behind and saw nothing I decided to have a long look at the handsome chap sitting there. It  was me. What grace, what elegance, what ears, what glossy fur and such a happy twitching nose. Funny how it keeps going by itself. I don't do anything special. I'm not too sure about the back view though. Does my bum look big?

Genuis or instinct

Every day brings a new problem for me to identify and solve. Take these dark mornings. J, my primary care giver gets up early, gives me a greeting snip of carrot and has a cup of tea. M, my second in command thinks it's still night time and doesn't move. Now this could affect my breakfast, so I need to work out a way of getting him downstairs and slotted into place as food provider number two in case my number one decides to have an early bath and forgets my breakfast. It has been known but I don't hold grudges.

For a vertically challenged rabbit like me there are several important moves to get straight. First, the door to the hall needs to be opened. I sit and stare at it until J gets the message then take a long, calculated look at the first step of the staircase. Will I be able to jump that high without bumping my head on the next step? Which foot goes first? I can never remember.

Staircase secured. Next there is the mad scamper to the top followed by a quick decision whether to turn right or left. There he lies as usual under a rose

February

covered eiderdown. I give a few tugs at this with my teeth. When he doesn't budge, your mountaineering hero thumps! A mumble comes from underneath the blankets. "Ok, Harve, you win." Plan executed with success.

Using information to reach a conclusion would be called problem solving by humans. They would claim it as intelligence and their prerogative. What arrogant nonsense. When I do a thing for the first time I decide on a plan, work out how to do it then put it into action. On one hand there is nature which includes things I would need to know in the wild where survival comes first then at home there is nurture where training my family comes first. Why would I want to know how to get a human out of bed if I were a wild rabbit? Have you ever spotted a human asleep by a rabbit hole in a field with a packet of my favourite crunchies in his hand? Of course not! No, I work out my problems all by myself as they come up.

Mice and the hole

There's never a dull moment in our house. This morning we found a hole in my bag of dry food on the pantry floor. "Mice," squealed J. "There's rabbit food everywhere." She's been a bit funny about mice since Figgi the cat died. Packets, boxes, jars and tins flew off the shelves and were put down on the floor for me to check. The cornflakes needed extra attention to make sure they tasted the same and there was nobody hiding inside. You never can tell with mice.

"Not a sign of a single mouse," she announced when everything had been put back. I could have told her that. I know who nibbled the hole but I'm not telling.

My two friends Spike and Poppy are in trouble as well. They have learned how to escape from their overnight den and sleep in the sitting room beside the fire. Somebody had chewed holes in the fireside rug overnight and they got the blame. Nobody could be sure

February

they saw them do it but it's easier to blame Spike and Poppy than Edward the baby who only has one tooth.

House rabbits have to take a lot of blame where chewing is concerned. I wouldn't say I've been responsible for much damage in my house. I chewed a bit of the television cupboard because the doors were closed and it was time for The Simpsons, frilled the edge of  the sofa arm cover to start an entrance to a burrow in case I needed an escape route in a hurry and neatened the carpet fringe a smidgen. There was nothing that didn't need a bit of attention and it was all done very tastefully. They could have shown a bit more appreciation in my opinion.

Advice for bedtime

Apart from the carrot, these ideas should work for most house pets although I'm not sure about budgies.

1. Watch carefully for signs leading to bedtime and ask for a piece of carrot. This gives them confidence and they think you are ready for bed.
2. Eat carrot quickly then dash past them and make a run for the stairs.
3. Hide where they don't expect you to.
4. Keep as still as possible. Any movement can give your hiding place away. Don't make a lump under curtains or bedspread.
5. Try not to get impatient. They will sometimes pretend they have stopped looking for you so stick it out.

Three things can happen now so get ready to use the following tactics. You might be found and they will try to chase you downstairs. This is easy to manage just dash underneath the nearest bed and keep edging away from groping hands. After about ten minutes they will be so annoyed they will put all lights out and pretend to go to bed. Stay where you are until you think they have dozed off then stamp your back foot over and over again as only a rabbit can until one of them comes to see what you are up to.

The worst scenario is, they will make a quick grab and carry you downstairs. I haven't worked out what to do about this so I usually act cute, stand on my back legs and tell them I haven't had my bedtime carrot. It usually works and you have had a lot of fun. I'm still not sure about budgies.

February

Cold weather

I had a peep outside today but it's still freezing. The birds are keeping an eye on things for me while they hang about on their dangling peanut cage. Damp and draughts are supposed to be worse for rabbits than cold but I keep away from it all. These experts are always doing research to prove something or other then somebody else pops up and proves the opposite. It's better to stick to your own rules I say. My family knows I like the fire to myself on chilly evenings. I stretch out to keep them away from my warm spot and if anyone gets in my way, squiggle myself in between them and the fire. A good way of moving them altogether is to concentrate on a patch of their bare skin and lick the same place over and over again. This irritates them for some reason so they soon move. Life with humans is easy if you choose the right kind. That's the hard bit, choosing the best. I try not to think about rabbits freezing in their hutches. People should have to pass exams before they are allowed to keep rabbits.

March

Is it spring?

I'm in a digging mood and feeling great. If I put an extra bit of effort into it I can scatter my litter yards from my tray while I find the right spot. Normally I just give a gentle scrabble before settling down but for some reason at the moment I want to throw it high in the air like confetti.

Because I'd been giving my litter so much attention they thought I might have cystitis but I haven't. It's just exuberance.

It's the same with my bed. Usually a bit of a tug this way and that puts it into place but now I want to toss my cuddle blankets as far away as I can. My hay bag is the best thing for digging practice. In go the front legs, scrabbling hard then the back legs do a quick flick and out the hay flies in a great cloud. Every scrabble and kick is very satisfying. With hard work it's soon empty. House rabbits should always have a hay bag. Every sitting room needs one to add a bit of homeliness.

All this is very good exercise for me but there's something else I can't put my paw on. I feel a bit more excited than usual and there's something at the back of my mind and deep inside telling me I need to organise things in preparation for something. The problem is I don't know what.

The old cat basket trick

This was definitely not the thing at the back of my mind! Can you believe it? There I was, dozing happily under my table, listening to the rain battering on the windows while I dreamt of a sunny field full of dandelions and clover when without any warning I was scooped up, plonked in the old cat basket and dumped in the car. Great! I knew exactly what was happening. It would be a visit to the vet. Just the thing I hadn't planned on for the day. My absolute un-favourite happening and not a thing I could do about it.

The journey there was bearable. I spent it making the basket more comfortable by tugging and scrabbling my blankets and pulling them about with my teeth until I arranged it to my liking. When it was time to see my

March

doctor, Simon, I'd prepared myself for the worst and couldn't keep my back legs from trembling. The weigh-in wasn't too bad. I was perfect as usual. The stomach prodding was ticklish then he peered unceremoniously at my rear end. None of it was scary until he decided to check my teeth. That was horrible. He held my mouth wide open and shone his torch at everything in there. It lasted for ever. "Do his snuffles get any worse than this?" he asked. Snuffles? I wasn't snuffling. I was making the loudest 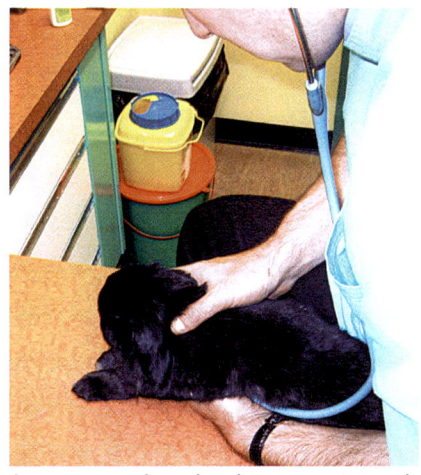 noise I could with my mouth jammed wide open and a whacking great torch stuffed inside. J explained for me. "Ah," he said, "It's just for my benefit is it?" Too right! Who else would I be complaining about? They say only one third of a bunny's teeth can be seen easily but my specialist vet knows how to see more.

Not a hair was left unturned and to crown it all there was the myxie jab. As a matter of fact I didn't feel a thing but what would have been the point arguing anyway? Just as I was breathing a sigh of relief at being put back in my basket I was whipped out again and my toe nails were attacked. I don't know what I would have done if he had decided to trim my beautiful whiskers.

The old cat basket felt comfortable and cosy on the way home and thinking about it now, I quite enjoyed the change. I had a ride out, met some friendly people and my vet always gives me a cuddle and chats to me when it's all over. I'm very lucky because he specialises only in cats and rabbits so there are never any other animals around to alarm or startle me.

The art of back turning

I did not do it! It wasn't me because I wasn't there. Somebody had spilled my hay all over the sitting room carpet and I got the blame as usual. There is only one thing a rabbit can do in such circumstances and that is, turn his back. If they try to blame you for something, turn your back. If you want to object to anything at all, turn your back and sit tight. It might seem a bit rude at first but it's the only solution when you can't make the sounds humans make. Back turning is an art because once you have done it you have to stick to your guns. If you give way when they wave a piece of carrot under your nose you have lost the argument.

March

They were still a bit grumpy while I was rootling around in my litter tray trying to sort a place to settle. "Must you make such a racket Harvey? We're trying to listen to the weather forecast?" For goodness sake, can't they look out of the window at the weather? Digging a reasonable hole in my litter is essential and it takes time. Anyway, I like the noise it makes and it keeps me in training in case I ever want to do a bit of scrape making in the garden. It's my ritual and rabbits need ritual. Whose house is this anyway?

A day in my life

You will be well up to speed with the fact my primary care giver doesn't know enough about house bunnies yet. The new training sessions are not going as well as I'd planned. Take yesterday for instance.

7.30 am. J comes downstairs. I dash backwards and forwards, give her a lick to try to convince her it's really 9.30 am and time for my breakfast. No luck.

8 am. Get under her feet and trip her up when she goes for another cup of tea. Tell her again it is 9.30 am. I'm ignored so sit in the utility room and stare hard at my empty bowl. It has no effect.

9 am. I run in circles round her feet and trip her up again. She is still quite sleepy. Nothing happens.

9.25 am. Fed up. Decide I may as well have a nap.

9.45 am. Somebody whistles! At last! Sixteen grams of crunchy deliciousness rattle into my bowl. I eat too quickly and flop out under the table until things shuffle down.

11 am. Very wet day so I'm allowed upstairs to play. Find newspaper at side of bed so decide to help with tidying.

12 noon. Finish sorting newspaper. Exhausted but very, very pleased with the result. Get no thanks for expertise and am chased downstairs. Sleep most of the afternoon with time off for grass and hay.

5 pm. Have good wash. Manage to get ends of ears into mouth. All ready for television.

6 pm. Television time! Do not disturb until I am ready for family play. You see my problem?

March

A hutch is not enough for a rabbit

I've been thinking a lot about other rabbits during these cold months while I snooze beside the fire. I wish they could all have snug homes like me or lovely garden houses like my friend Viola Rose. She lives with her large family and every summer their rabbit friendly garden is open to raise money for less happy buns living in rescue places. They have big comfortable houses, bonded partners and masses of space to hop and run and jump and binky whenever they feel like it. We rabbits need a family with somebody to love and care for us exactly the same as other companion animals like dogs and cats. Small hutches are very cruel. Rabbits need more than a hutch.

March

The importance of feet

Body language is more important to a house rabbit than it would be to a hutch rabbit. Take feet watching for instance. If I had to pick out one of the most important activities in my life it would be watching feet.

I keep a wary eye on them most of the day except when I'm asleep. Feet can tell you exactly what goes on about the house. You know what your family is doing and why. They are going out when their feet head for the door or if feet go into the utility room it's always worth following in case fridge and carrots are involved. If feet wander towards the sitting room the television might be switched on so it's time for me to get a good seat between my hay bag and the screen. Doorways are probably the best place to feet watch.

Hands will be more important to a hutch rabbit because they bring food and water and clean out the place. Now, I'm not too keen on hands. They pick you up and check things out. No, I'm a feet man myself.

The living is easy

I have found outside again so decided to have an adventure this morning. There was so much to tidy up around the back door. I had a look at my parsley pot but not much was happening so I hopped up the steps to loosen the soil ready for planting my beans and carrot seeds. Some mallard ducks decided to visit so I did a couple of very high binkies and they left in a hurry. That showed them whose garden it is.

I was still in a tidying mood when I went back inside so started on the carpet fringe. My usual stretch had disappeared. I'm sure I didn't nibble through that amount. Maybe it has been tucked under for a reason but it seemed a bit odd.

After such a full morning, my afternoon was spent napping to gather strength for tomorrow. Who knows what's in store. I'm going to doze and make plans.

April

Sad goodbyes

My friend Teasel has died. I'm putting it in my diary to help me remember. His family told us how much he was loved.

"Teasel was the most stunningly intelligent, gentle, handsome and mischievous rabbit - my own favourite who lived with us for over eight years after coming from Wood Green Animal Sanctuary. He had three girl friends, Florence, Sage and Robinia each of whom fell in love with him at first sight. He is survived by Robinia. We are devastated."

I know you will worry about your family, Teasel. They will find it hard to manage without you. Binky free and give my love to the Great White Rabbit on Rainbow Bridge.

Not again please

In case all my friends think I have an easy life and I live like a lord, that I'm a spoilt rabbit who doesn't appreciate his luxurious lifestyle, take a look at this.

They call this de-fluffing. I have carefully pointed out to them on many occasions that I will not be groomed with a brush so what do they do? They grab me while I'm in dozing heaven, hoist me onto the bench, hold me down in a half nelson with one hand and have the temerity to yank out great clumps of my beautiful powder-puff fur with the other. What is even

worse they were shown how to do this by my vet, the man I thought was my friend. The very man every rabbit should turn to at least twice a year to keep itself fit and well. Think again friends. Then I saw this photograph of a rabbit in a snowy garden with his myxie eye, desperately nibbling a tasteless Elaeagnus bush because he was so very hungry and I pulled my cuddle blankets over my head and counted my blessings. Moulting time is nothing in the great scheme of things is it?

April

Bonjour Mimi

I'm so excited! I've been invited to visit my pen-pal, half-a-tail-Mimi who lives in a ninth floor apartment in Paris. Naturally she is a house cat. She lost part of her tail on the streets before she was rescued.

Our humans keep in touch for us so we know what the other one is up to. Living indoors means we do the same sort of things like eating regularly, sleeping, hiding in various places, getting under feet and entertaining guests so we have a lot in common. I'd say I am more helpful around the house. Mimi doesn't get so involved with what goes on and prefers to watch from a distance. The other morning she knocked over a vase of flowers and spilt water on the lovely wood floor. Then she paddled in it and tried to drink it but she made too much noise and was discovered.

If I decide to go I wouldn't know what to wear. This beret is chic and very French but would Mimi be more impressed by English city style? And should I take champagne or onions?

It was my vet who said I should go abroad for a change to make my diary more interesting so I've been thinking about what I might do when I get there. A few touristy things would be good. Maybe a boat trip on the river or I could sun myself on Paris Plage. They do a good salad in Paris. Mimi would eat the olives for me. I tried to explain to her about catmint being the thing for cats but between you and me I think she needs to join her local branch of

April

Olives Anonymous. As you know, I'm in complete control of temptation apart from dandelion leaves, rocket, valerian, carrots, banana, raisins and other delicious things that might accidentally get in my way at ground level but Mimi climbs on the table to steal olives then leaves them all over the floor.

Still, it might be nice to visit her for a change of scenery.

Tea time

I wrecked my cardboard box today and scrabbled my dozing mats into a messy heap. It felt really good when I had finished, sort of satisfying. Usually I don't mind when they go out because it means I can sleep undisturbed but when it came round to salad time this afternoon and there was nothing in my dish I had a bit of a tantrum. There was my dried grass which isn't bad on the whole but there's a time and place for it and 5-o-clock in the afternoon is not it. That's the slot for juicy green grass and herbs. I like things in my day to be regular. I'm quite old now so I deserve more consideration.

Nothing much has changed over the years. I still have a fine head of hair and healthy teeth. I'm not overweight and my running speed is up to scratch. I can come to a halt on a five pence piece and binky if I feel like it. I might take more naps and I like to take time over my breakfast instead of rushing through it but that's all. They would say I nag more often but I do get urges for carrot and banana. It should be every hour on the hour but they don't understand. What good is carrot and banana once a day?

In hiding

I've just come out of hiding saved once again by the forest of table and chair legs in the kitchen. Why was I hiding? The signals I recognise for poop-check time sent me diving for cover. I can tell things are getting dangerous when they both come into the utility room at food time. If they shut the door there is no escape and I have to suffer being picked up while my personal bits are inspected. Usually a quick check is all I need but if I have missed out on a quick

April

lick at wash and brush-up time they might decide to snip a bit of fur and use the blue bunny flannel. That's when I complain. We rabbits are supposed to be silent creatures but let me tell you I can grumble and grouse with the best of them. I can sing too as I hop along when I'm happy which is most of the time. Then I can do a special sort of tooth grind when J is cuddling me on the floor. It's a kind of purr and you could feel it under my chin if I let you. Wash and brush-up time is not on my list of favourites.

Hello, somebody is whistling. That means food. At this time of day it's juicy grass. They put it in my hay bowl but I can pick out every single blade without touching anything else. Got to go and enjoy.

Battle stations

They've tried it on again. There's been another hay invasion into my bowl of grassy herbs but it failed miserably thanks to your hero. I like my dandelion grass and I'm used to it because it's a nice, comfortable size for my mouth. I can snuggle my nose into it without getting prickled by ends of hay while I rest my chin in it and munch. It's sorted now. I picked every bit out of my bowl overnight while they weren't there to interfere. I wonder if they will notice and take the hint.

There are some things I can't do anything about. No matter how much I object at the time they still take me to see my vet. I bounce, I sing, I eat, drink and keep myself clean. I'm a happy, healthy, sober, elderly bun but they still do it. Have they got money to burn?

I'm never going to grumble again though because today I met Roger. Roger is deaf and he has had a stroke. Now he has a sore eye where they think some dust or maybe a sharp piece of hay has scratched it yet Roger is a lucky bun because his human mum loves him very, very much. He adores being nursed and cuddled as often as possible while he lies blissfully in his mum's arms and will probably be able to feel her heart beating and the vibrations of her voice when she talks to him. He has his own duvet beside a heater so he is warm and cosy in cold weather.

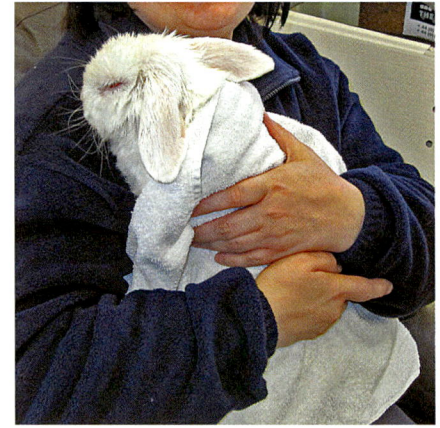

I thank the Great White Rabbit in the sky for my health and happiness.

May

Ready for summer

Mr. Sparkle came to clean my kitchen rug today. I tried to help him but was scooped up and put in another room. Somebody always spoils my fun. Pulling his sheets into reasonable order would have improved matters and made the job easier for him because organising covers is one of my specialities. I'm an excellent bed  maker. He made a joke about me being a soft toy then said he meets lots of house rabbits who jump out at him when he least expects it. I was pleased about that. Jumping out at people is another of my specialities.

There's always a sniff of bad news in the air at this time of year and my rear end is being inspected more than once a day which means the dreaded Rearguard is imminent. I hate Rearguard. It makes me feel poorly for a couple of days or so. It's the fault of all those chemicals I expect but I can't escape it. When I wash myself I can't help licking the stuff. I only have it in warm weather when there might be flies about.

I told you so

I knew it. I knew it. I've been to have the dreaded Rearguard and have been huffing with my face towards the wall for hours. I tried to hide up J's jumper while the vet was putting the stuff on but only managed to get my head in with my rear sticking out. How did he know where I was when he couldn't see my face? Darn clever these cat and rabbit specialists. Anyway, it's over and done with so I can relax without worrying about being eaten alive by maggots. I wonder if it is only sheep and bunnies who have the fly strike problem. There was extra parsley and rocket afterwards. Anything with a strong flavour takes the taste of Rearguard away. I might even get a sniff of banana later this evening.

Ducks

I'm not jealous but everybody is talking about that mallard in my garden so I'm huffing. In spite of all my warnings she came back and stayed. All I hear is,

May

"Is she off her nest yet?" "Has she come for food this morning?" "Have the drakes visited today?" It's nothing but ducks, ducks, ducks all day long.

I went outside yesterday to check for myself. It's my garden for goodness sake even though I don't bother with it much. You can't cover everything when you're a house rabbit but that doesn't mean I want other folk poking their noses into my affairs. I did my usual checking to see whether my carrot seeds were sprouting, trimmed the parsley again and peered into one or two of the borders but didn't spot or smell her. She must be well hidden. There was nobody in the pond either. I'll be glad when those chicks hatch and we can get back to me being centre stage. It can't be too long now. Wonder what she's up to?

Ouch!

That duck has bitten me! She has a huge mouth. All I did was to wander over to see what she was eating and she pecked me. I only wanted to taste the stuff they put in a dish for her. She's very uppity since she laid her eggs although we still don't know where they are. Surely she must know the babies won't be able to get out of the garden because we have walls and fencing all round to keep intruders out. At least the dogs and cats I've lived with had more sense and didn't lay eggs in other people's gardens. It's the ducklings I feel sorry for, having such a silly mother.

J is a bit worried now in case I catch a duck disease because of the mess in the yard. She doesn't use a litter tray you know. The duck I mean, not my primary care giver.

That bossy blackbird is nagging for grapes and sultanas. Has nobody told him about worms? Worms are for blackbirds and sultanas are for rabbits. He has at least one baby who comes onto my patch.

Unloved

I'm feeling a bit gloomy today. Nobody has taken any notice of me for what seems like weeks. Oh, they give me food and water and stuff but they don't love me the way they did before the duck invasion. I was just thinking about leaving home when suddenly, after spending all that time in the flower border, Daisy appeared followed by ten balls of feathery fluff with enormous feet and beaks just like hers. They won't have any trouble recognising their mother.

May

Because there are so many cats in the neighbourhood, especially a mean black and white one known as the duck filled catypus, we, not me, decided to keep them until they grow strong enough to walk down the lane to the lake.

It was Disney World here for them. They ate chick crumbs every couple of hours, washed them down with fresh water, dashed maniacally about the garden and nibbled everything in sight including my carrot tops. They pooped all over the yard, plopped in and out of the pond, fell down the side of the oil tank and had to be fished out with the pond net while Daisy quacked and fussed around in panic.

It went on and on while they grew bigger and bigger, then three days in a row they escaped into the big garden. Great, I thought, Molly the cat next door will get them but they came back each day for lunch, slept over, ate like horses then escaped again for good.

After that we needed a rest so I went to Bunny Hops while the family went to the seaside.

Bunny Hops is one of my favourite places in the world. I was fussed and cuddled and had a bedtime story every night with my carrot. I took all my own stuff so it was home from home. Naturally they love me. I needed to leave quite a lot of my droppings around my den to make it really mine because there were one or two other rabbits about but I don't think Julie minded the extra work. She sent a text to my family twice a day with pictures. I love it there because so much happens on the entertainment front and best of all it's a duck free haven.

June

A pet of my own

Now the weather is warmer I've been thinking about spending a bit more time outdoors. Just thinking about it mind you because I'm not sure what I used to do outside last year. There was my herb garden and lots of chairs to sit under to shelter from the sun but I can't see them now. Nope, I've forgotten. It all looks too big out there so don't think I'll bother although I can spot one of my dandelions growing in a crack in the pavement.

I'm settled on 16 grams of pellet food a day now. Any less and I lose weight at my age. All the vitamins and minerals I need are there and I have a huge pile of greens to keep my digestive system ticking over nicely. Then it's hay, a few mixed herbs with fresh grass for tea and then my evening carrot with a taste of fruit, maybe apple or pear. Not a bad day's supply all in all and I've put on a couple of grams in weight too because my bowel is working properly. Just in case they forget to feed me at the right time I always give a few tugs at M's trousers while he is having breakfast until he gets the message. He's quite bright really for a person. In fact they both understand my contact language

pretty well. It didn't take nearly as long to train my dog, Willow when I lived with her. A couple of bites on her nose did the trick.

Some friends of mine have their own tortoise. A tortoise can be very useful for finding dandelions then all you need to do is to grab the flower out of its mouth. It's quite easy because they eat slowly. I might ask for a tortoise for my birthday this year.

Cushions and me

It's been another busy day in front of the camera. A famous designer came to take pictures of me to use on cushions. I was photographed from all angles so she could get the feel of a rabbit. Of course she had to admit I looked good from all sides but I let her get on with it and sat as still as I could. She wondered what the bit sticking out was when she looked at me sideways. It was my nose! I know it's pretty flat but that was taking things a bit too far. Mind you, I'm

June

used to the things humans come out with but it amazes me each time.

Still, it was worth it because I now have my very own cushion. It's soft and velvety and smells new and I love it. This is going to be my special seat from now on. I can even watch television from here.

Square eggs

I think I've heard everything now. I was keeping a close watch on my space to make sure everything was put back in exactly the same spot on my mat while my second in command was doing a bit of a clean up when he suddenly said, "Why can't this rabbit make square droppings so they won't roll around all over the place?"

Well, to start with, the droppings as he calls them are not done on purpose. They seem to spill a bit when I jump out of my litter tray and secondly this rabbit has a name. Anyway, I make them this way because it's more comfortable for me. Does he ask hens to lay square eggs? How would he get his spoon into the corners if eggs were square? If I grumble too much they might decide to get a sleeping cage for me overnight and I wouldn't like that at all so best to keep quiet and pretend I don't understand what they say. I love sleeping under my kitchen table. It's my events arena as well as my safety zone. I keep watch over family life from under there and perfect my jumping skills. It's my own play room.

June

Midsummer

We had rain on midsummer day and it was a bit blustery so I stayed home to look after things while the others went to visit our friend Twigs and her family of eighteen rabbits, some hens and a couple of tortoises and to nibble on some carrot cake and smell the roses in their lovely garden. Parsley is a very sensible chap and when the rain hurtled down he dashed for shelter and watched things from the comfort of his garden house. Wet paws and fur are not for me either.

I had news of them all. Damson is recovering nicely after his operation to remove a kidney stone but was resting in the nursery sick bay to make sure he didn't get underfoot. Viola Rose was looking beautiful again now she has recovered from her Myxie attack. It was an uphill struggle even though she always has her vaccination every six months. Twigs and Steve had planned to go on holiday but the morning they were due to leave Viola Rose went to them and showed them her streaming eyes and nose so they unpacked their suitcase and stayed with her. Her great love is Mistletoe Snowgoose. He was bought from a pet shop when he was very small. The pet shop owner said he would be perfectly happy living alone in a hutch on a balcony. Well, how silly is that? Six months later he turned into a large, powerful, hormonal fury. Not the pet shop owner – Mistletoe Snowgoose. Anyway, after one or two problems somebody told his family about Twigs because Twigs knows how rabbits should be kept.

One thing is a bit of a worry though. Steve sent me a message to say bought packets of curly kale might not be good for me in case it's not clean enough. I'm eating my own from the garden at the moment but will make sure anything bought from a shop is washed thoroughly before going into my bowl even when it says "washed and ready for use."

June

Back at last

I've been very, very poorly and had to stay in hospital. It was my dodgy digestive system again. I couldn't eat and couldn't poo and couldn't drink my water and had a terrible pain in my stomach. Whatever position I tried to sit in it hurt and I couldn't get it to stop. Thank goodness J notices everything so she took me straight to the vet. He gave me morphine and put me on a drip. Then I had to be rehydrated under my skin and fed with a syringe of complete food at frequent intervals. It was awful.

We rabbits have a complicated digestive system with masses of bowel and if we stop eating it means there is something very, very wrong. When I eventually got home I managed a dandelion leaf, a bit of rocket and a smidgeon of carrot. M and J were very excited when they saw me eating so I joined in the fun and ran around the furniture. In fact I was a bit naughty that night and wouldn't go to bed when told. I didn't care because I felt so well. Next day I started on my crunchies and I'm better now. I hope it doesn't happen again. Even my vet was worried. "It was touch and go," he said to my family afterwards. M, my second in command is just a people doctor so he isn't much good in bunny emergencies but he has been doing all he can by keeping my stuff squeaky clean just in case it was something I ate by mistake. The downside is I have to be weighed every few days in a microwave tub. I feel so silly.

What bliss to be able to stretch out under my table again, without pain. Life is good.

July

I've always known I am special

I've been thinking back to the day I had my first e-mail from Las Vegas and wondering how some humans can be so silly. It read, Dear Harvey, would you like to explore a career as a Forensic Scientist or Law Enforcement Officer? The second temptingly offered a momentous slim down....I could lose six pounds in two days while a third letter promised to help me buy property in the tropical paradise of Costa Rica. Unbelievably, one final e-mail was addressed to The Rabbitt Family. Somebody over there definitely needs a rabbit to provide education and training.

My family blocked my incoming mail after that. Not because they doubted my capabilities to do these jobs brilliantly but nobody wanted me to emigrate to take up a position so far away from home. I'm much too useful around the house. My vet offered to check out the Costa Rica paradise for me. It was kind of him but they all wondered how someone had managed to break into our computer system in spite of all our protection. Mistaking me for a person was ridiculous too. Maybe they don't know about rabbits in America.

The best thing ever which proved how really special I am, was a dedication to me in my friend Celia's book, "One Hundred Ways to a Happy Bunny." I'm very proud of that. It says "This book is dedicated to Harvey, an inspirational house bunny." How special can one rabbit be!

Birthday portrait

It's my birthday! The family seems very excited and keep singing to me. I wonder how old I am in human terms. Do I times by seven or ten? If it's ten then I'm ninety but if it's seven I'm only ... umm ... it might be sixty four. No, that can't be right, it sounds like a song. I don't care which it is. I'm still as fit as a fiddle and can jump as high as a kite, binky like a kitten and run as fast as ... a rabbit. There's always plenty of practice for this sort of thing in my house.

July

I agreed to have a birthday portrait taken but only on condition they wouldn't groom me beforehand. Not for a hundred birthday portraits will I allow it. I don't mind my head and ears brushed gently but not further down my back thank you very much. We buck rabbits have our pride. Doe buns might like to be titivated to attract good looking chaps like me but not yours truly. Anyway, rabbits don't get fur balls like cats, not very often anyway.

Nine or ten is a good age for a rabbit. My cousins in the wild rarely live longer than eighteen months, or so I read in a book.

This is my pensive look by the way. I think M has caught it quite well.

Napping is definitely on my agenda today when I have finished checking my present list. At my age you can nap as often as you like

Now, did I get everything I asked for?

1. One whole banana just for me.

2. One whole large carrot, just for me all at once.

3. One piece of carrot cake with extra-large juicy raisins.

4. One packet of cornflakes, the kind with sugar and nuts.

5. One ripe pear.

6. One ripe peach.

7. One bouquet garni of mint, parsley, dandelion leaves and rocket.

8. One whole day when I don't hear the word, NO.

Hello, where's my carrot cake?

I've blown it!

I have blown it and don't know what to do to put things right. Last night, on the sofa I lost control completely and upset the most important woman in my life. It began so innocently. She had given me a bit of her banana and I desperately wanted more but no matter how beautifully I sang and shivered my back legs she wouldn't listen. In my frustration I turned my back and sprayed the sofa, the wretched banana and her. There

July

was a loud screech and I was picked up and carried, carried mind you, to my litter tray in the utility room. Imagine my humiliation. I tossed and turned all night long while I tried to make sense of it all. I remember spraying in the garden years ago and on a pile of old gardening shoes where I like to sit and camouflage myself but never anywhere else and never since my operation.

I have stayed under the kitchen table most of today and slept a lot. Nobody has been down to talk to me yet so I am very doubtful about being allowed to watch television tonight. There will be no sofa sitting that's for sure.

Compliments

The nicest compliment I ever had was paid to me by one of my doctors, Kim. "I love his little front legs," she said. Now, you might not think this is a big deal but when I tell you Kim came from Australia you will see the magnificence of the words and the magnitude of the compliment. Australians are not generally big on rabbits. It's an historical fact. I think in some states people are banned from keeping bunnies as pets. There's an Australian House Rabbit Society so maybe somebody reading this could let me know.

Kim said she couldn't believe the popularity of pet rabbits when she first came here. She and her husband Simon are famous cat and rabbit specialists. If a rabbit can win over an Australian with his little front legs, there is nothing he can't do.

Toys

I would like to state categorically and especially bun-egorically to rabbit experts of the world, I do not like toys. I see no point in a rope carrot ... what a disappointment ... or a plastic jingle ball or a cardboard box full of bits for scrabbling. I mean, why am I scrabbling? To what end? I don't need look for food. If I want a treat I sit in my basket on my back legs beside the fridge and they can't resist that.

A few weeks ago I found a cardboard box filled with shredded paper in the utility room, a place I use for breakfast and for my litter but why would I want

July

to spend time there when I can have adventures around the rest of the house?

I did my bit for them, naturally. I looked at it then turned my back which should have been a big enough hint but J picked me up and plonked me in it. I sat there, nibbled a piece of paper, put it down and jumped out. Who would give up a cosy rug, television and the possibility of finding a delicious cornflake in the kitchen in exchange for an old cardboard box full of shredded paper in a utility room? I don't think so. It's not on my list of things I must include in my life.

You might be forgiven for thinking I'm playing if you see me flicking through the pages of a book left on the floor. That's one of my many neat tricks but I'm really just checking the plot to make sure it is suitable reading for my primary care giver. A newspaper is fine to sit on for a few minutes while I frill the edges and I can sniff out a bit of carrot in a cardboard roll in a second. You pick up one end and the carrot rolls out the other. Where's the skill in that? A paper towel screwed up can hide a juicy raisin or two but if it has been scrunched too tightly and I can't undo it, well, why bother? Back to the television I say.

The bottom line here is, I do not do floor shows with shop bought items. I like to make up my own games. When we have visitors I am willing to help with the entertaining. I scrabble around under the curtain puddle which I use as my indoor burrow and stick my head out now and again to surprise them. That goes down well and I always follow them into the hall when they leave to help them on their way. These are small things a well mannered house rabbit should do but playing with a rope carrot? No thanks. Please do not underestimate my intelligence.

Another good idea

One thing this old bun has learned is if you want to train your human family, you need to re-adjust your own mind set. Forget about being a lagomorph. That's for wild rabbits to boast about. For a house rabbit like me, stamping is no longer a sign for danger. My cousins in the wild need it but for me foot stamping is for getting immediate attention and it works brilliantly. A sharp

July

whack on the floor with my back leg moves them straight into action. We rabbits can communicate with one another worldwide with a few thumps.

Last night when I had nothing better to do, I decided to experiment on a way to get the old folk upstairs and early to bed so I hopped up to their room. I know exactly where they sleep when they leave me alone downstairs overnight. Sometimes I potter along to my bedroom for a bit of peace but this time I had something on my mind. I gave a few superb stamps on the floor above them as only a rabbit can and waited. As sure as eggs are eggs J came dashing up to see what the problem was. I stared hard at her and held my statue position until she got the message and lay down on the bed then I ran over and flopped out beside her for the night. Done, I thought, feeling very pleased with myself. That was the successful part. Suddenly, not at all according to my plan and just as I had closed my eyes she leapt up, grabbed me and carried me downstairs. Not a perfect result but an achievement in part for rabbit kind. I wonder where I went wrong. I'm running out of new training ideas after all these years and feel they still don't fully understand me.

"I don't know why he does these things," J complained to M a bit later. I wonder what mischievous means.

A bit of a worry

There's a lot of whispering in the house today. They've discovered a lump in my groin and you'd think the world was coming to an end. They found it when they were giving me my wash and brush up this morning. It doesn't bother me in the least. I can still run and jump and scrabble my dozing mats but their faces look very serious at the moment. M thinks it's a hernia. Well, I'm an elderly guy like him but it seems rabbits who have had the operation don't get them on the whole. The problem is my specialist vet broke his leg skateboarding with his son and isn't working at the moment. I'm going to have a word with him about growing old gracefully when I see him. I'm lucky because Kim, his wife is a rabbit specialist as well so everything will be alright. What a muddle. I'm not in the least bothered though. I know I feel fine.

Phew, back home again. Panic over and all is well. I tore a muscle and a lump came up. It's only a traumatic hernia after all. I knew I felt ok. I saw both my vets, Kim as well as Simon who had come in on his crutches so had a huge amount of attention. They said it wouldn't be advisable to operate because it would be like trying to stitch tissue paper to butter so I have to take things easy and not do any more Geronimo jumps from the sofa for the time being. Will I be able to resist temptation?

July

Companion animals like me are very sensible about these things on the whole. We don't have to go hunting for food so we sleep a lot when we don't feel well. I don't binky much at my age anyway. Binkying is for younger rabbits.

Wellingtons and water wings

What a palaver this morning. The fridge-freezer where my carrots are kept broke down during the night and the utility floor was flooded. None of my stuff was wet but J seemed a bit over agitated. "How can you sit there calmly doing the crossword and eating cornflakes while the rabbit is paddling around in wellies and water wings?" she said crossly to M. I wasn't, of course, I was under the kitchen table waiting for the odd crunchy, nutty flake to fall in my direction. Anyway, I don't wear water wings. She can exaggerate at times.

There was a load of sorting to do when everything was dry. Nudging my dishes back into place if they are put in a different order is easy enough. Everything out of place at floor level is my responsibility. I like to have my bowls in exactly the right position. Dry food has to go on the right, then water then greens and last of all, my hay bowl.

They were still a bit manic after that and before I realised what was happening they grabbed me and started pulling at my loose fur. It was my fault for hanging around and not making my escape as soon as the mopping up was

July

finished so there was no point in grumbling. Flopping out and thinking about the treat I would be given afterwards seemed the only sensible course of action. Moulting time seems to be all the year round for me. I blame the warm house. My fur seems to fall out in winter as well as summer. It can be a bit scary watching the pile of my beautiful soft fur grow higher. As long as they leave some to cover my important places, I feel cooler afterwards and less itchy.

The trouble with life with humans is, if it's not moulting time its poop-check time or Rearguard time or weigh in time or injection time. Wild rabbits don't have this problem. Nothing like this is ever organised by me. I don't want to be too critical of my family but I've noticed that human beings have something in their nature which precludes them from remembering stuff really important to rabbits. What about carrots, bananas, pears, apples, herbs, dandelions, rose petals and cornflakes? These things should be printed in their genes like the colour of hair or eyes. Why can't important things be put first? That's what I think anyway and nobody could call me a fussy, furry person could they?

Bobbing for broccoli

The reason broccoli keeps appearing in my dish could be because J is getting old and forgetful or maybe my teaching methods are at fault. Whatever it is, I keep finding green stalks with bits on the end hidden under cabbage leaves. I love the crunchy green stalks but not the feel of the crumbly ends in my

mouth. My solution is to toss it out of my bowl when I find it. Anywhere will do as long as it doesn't get in the way of my teeth. My favourite vegetables are munched first then what's left I finish later but not broccoli or sprouts. Now, pea tops are good along with celery leaves, parsley and carrot tops then cabbage. Sweet cabbage, that is. I don't eat any old curly cabbage. Spring greens are good if they are fresh. I heard them telling somebody they have to make soup out of floppy greens left in the fridge because I don't like them. What's wrong with that? I get first choice then they eat the rest. That's the whole idea of having a pet isn't it? So why does J sniff and say, "You're like a two year old Harve, eating your favourite things first."

My cat friend Paris-Mimi agrees with this method. She always licks the gravy from her food first. She told me George Bush senior hates broccoli as well. If one of the presidents of America won't eat it why should I? He would be on my side I'm sure. I might write to him for support.

What is a happy bunny?

It's not difficult to tell when rabbits are happy. We have lots of ways to show it. A happy bunny is one ...

- Who runs to you with a kiss every morning
- Who dashes about the house ecstatically, leaping in the air as he runs
- Who pushes his face into your hand, sticks his nose between your fingers and leaves it there to show how much he loves you
- Who sings as he hops along when he hears the word carrot or banana
- Who makes a game of running out through one door and in through another until you speak to him or until he is tired
- Who confidently throws himself sideways in an attempt to roll over but never quite manages it because of his body shape
- Who introduces himself to visitors then shows them to the door when they leave
- Who stretches out at your feet every evening just to be close.
- Who makes a nightly sofa circuit to tell you he is going to bed.

These are some of the ways I use anyway.

August

Keeping squeaky clean

When I'm cleaning myself I won't speak to anybody. Even if the Queen came she would have to wait until I finish if she wanted to attract my attention. The only time I might be a bit weak willed is when I smell banana but it would have to be right under my nose to have an effect on me because cleaning is a very serious business and it takes first place after visits to my litter tray. When I'm satisfied with the job and smelling of rabbit I finish with a long stretch. Now and again to get my legs back in order I might walk a few steps instead of hopping. The first time J noticed this she was very excited. "He's walking on all four legs," she squealed. Well, what else would I walk on for goodness sake? I'll need to be more circumspect another time. I worry when she gets too excited. It's not good for her and I need undivided attention for years to come. Anyway, you can't get up much speed when you walk. Your rear end tends to stick up in the air instead of being tucked up neatly behind.

What else has been happening? Oh, yes, yesterday I found one of the most delicious things to put on my list of favourite foods. It's called a digestive biscuit. It was sitting casually on a plate on the floor waiting for me so I took it. I could tell it was meant for me because it smelled of cereal and sugar. J knows they are my favourite things so why did she get agitated and chase me as I ran off with it? The bad thing about digestive biscuits is the way they fall apart so I only managed a small nibble after all. Life can be very unfair at times. Still, it's another thing to dream about.

Cold feet

My table is wearing socks! Yes, really. It gave me a bit of a surprise so I sidled up to it, sniffed and wandered around a couple of times in case I was seeing things but socks they were. It must be a new fashion statement for furniture. I've heard the Victorians put skirts on their tables to hide the legs but this is ridiculous. I wonder why they're there. I liked those wooden feet. They were a bit tasty. It wouldn't matter so much if the socks matched

August

but they don't. I might try to pull them off when nobody is looking. It works well with human feet and I've had plenty of practice. I told one of my best friends about it. He's the blue dust catcher who picks up any bits I have mislaid. He makes an interesting noise when he talks and I always run to find him when he starts chatting. He's probably a relation of some sort because he smells just like me. Anyway, he had nothing to say about the socks so I'm no further forward in solving the mystery.

Musings

Food is one of the most important things in life to me. I think about it most of the time. If it seems to be running out I beg. I learned how to beg very early on. It was all my family's fault by tempting me with tasty nibbles. Rabbits' teeth are made for munching and nibbling. You can spot wild rabbits nibbling dangerously by the roadside or garden rabbits nibbling on lawns but it's too slow for me. I like a good, tasty mouthful. With a mouthful you get more flavours. That's one of the best things about being a house bun, you can stuff as much grassy salad into your mouth as you want in one go because it's picked and put in a bowl for you. I shove my face and my front legs in, open my mouth as wide as possible and in it all goes. There's a patch of grass outside to keep my teeth busy but I never bother with it. If I stare at it for long enough somebody will get exasperated and cut some for me. They think I don't know how to get it myself. It's all a matter of knowhow.

If I spent all my hours nibbling how would I get through my daily chores? I mean even small things like making my bed and writing in my diary wouldn't get done. And who would wander in and clear the cobwebs from the dark corners of the inglenook where, I'm ashamed to tell you, nobody else ever goes?

Not me. I'd be nibbling all the time. It can't be done.

E mail from Canada

We had a letter from Niagara on the Lake today. "Come over and bring the little guy with you," it said. Little guy? What do they mean? Now, chap, I think is an acceptable English form of address although not Bunny-bun-bun or Harvey Nicks which I'm called sometimes and have to turn my back and ignore. Well, honestly, what do you think?

August

When visitors come for the first time and spot me flopping out in front of the television they say things like, "Oh look, a rabbit." That's what I am so it's ok but what did they expect, an Aardvark? Or they say, "Where's its hutch?" That's another non-starter. After spending some time under the table with me another family friend announced, "He's a Cog!" He had noticed very cleverly for a human that rabbits clean themselves like cats and are hospitable like dogs but that's where it ends. There is so much more to a rabbit than that. I am vegetarian so I don't smell the way dogs do and I

can't be sick like cats. Rabbits don't leave sticky messes all over the lawn for humans to pick up. We are very neat where our deposits are concerned. Pretty perfect eh?

No, a lot of care should be taken when choosing a name for a house bunny. Buster is quite manly I think. So is Fred. On the whole, people who have house rabbits are very sensible about names. If I become more famous I might change my name to Napoleon or Nelson. Either one would suit my personality.

By the way, something new has been stuck on the wall beside my food dishes. I think it says, Home Sweet Home. That's nice.

Forgetfulness

I see my cardboard roll is back again thank goodness. I thought I'd lost it. Couldn't find it behind the sofa or in my curtain hideaway and had just about given up when there it was in the middle of the floor in front of the television where I usually flop out. Best of all it still had some carrot inside after all this time. It took me a moment or two to remember how to flick one end up in the air then look to see what had fallen out. To start with I thought my carrot came out from the end I flick but then realised I have to go to the other end where it falls out to find it. They always make me work it out for myself. I wonder if they have remembered about my screwed up paper towel with one or two raisins inside. I haven't seen that for ages. That makes for a very good scrabble. If I scratch the carpet a few times it might jog their memory.

September

A change of scenery

We're having a break for a few days while the weather is good. As usual, I had to lend a paw with the packing otherwise they would have taken far too much stuff. I tried to explain there are shops in Paris but it fell on deaf ears. Then a brilliant idea struck me. I could hide in the suitcase and jump out when we got there. The Paris newspapers would be all about me. "Arve le brave, le baggage binkying bunny arrives to visit Mimi," but I changed my mind when I remembered about frogs and snails. Frogs  and snails should be in the garden not in dishes thank you very much. A bit of crusty baguette can be tasty but not worth the journey. Anyway I will be going to Bunny Hops where I'll have a much better time.

There's a new hidey hole in the kitchen. It's a sort of tent with cushions inside. It must be for me. Although it looks cosy I'd rather be under my big table where I can see what's going on. I might investigate further when we get back.

Dotties in the house

Whatever you do never let a Dotty into your house. They have pins in their feet. We have one staying with us at the moment and the last few days have been a nightmare. It binkies in a fashion all over the place, ignores my foot stamping and has no sense of self discipline. It never stops bouncing and when it sees me, it wiggles its bottom and tries to jump at me. Worst of all it smells awful and its litter tray is disgusting. I couldn't have a child of mine making such a

September

mess. This particular Dotty was thrown away by somebody and I'm not surprised. House rules and the fact other folk might have opinions never enters its silly head. My first mum Joanne found it and took it home with her. Who knows why?

I had a close look at the Dotty while it was shut in a cage. It could be a sort of cat but I have never seen one so small. My family keeps it well away from my kitchen and utility room but I wish it would go away. I'm really depressed and try to sleep most of the time.

It has gone

It's gone. The Dotty has gone. Yes, yes, yes. It won't come here again that's for sure. It disgraced itself completely. My family knows how lucky it is to have a house rabbit. It peed on my curtain burrow and on the carpet in the corner of the room in spite of having two litter trays. It scratched all the chairs, chewed my diary and generally interfered with everything. M couldn't do his crossword in peace. It kept batting his pencil with its paws. Its batteries never ran down. I could hear them going even from the kitchen. What atrocious behaviour. What a mini tornado. I still feel shaky when I think about it. What if it escapes and finds its way back? I can feel my back legs beginning to quiver when I think about it. I had to check and sniff in every corner of the house to make sure it wasn't hiding in secret.

Marauders on the loose

Look what I found this morning on my garden path while I was sniffing around for a bit of dandelion leaf or an overlooked, ripe Victoria plum. Someone had committed murder in the night although I didn't hear a thing. Whoever it was and I have my suspicions about the cat next door, could have eaten some of the poor creature instead of just biting its head off and leaving it there for the flies. While the Dotty was staying here she caught three flies on the window but at least she ate them. I didn't say so but I was very proud of her because she was such a baby at the time. When I go outside it is usually to help with the daily chores not to kill somebody. At this time of year logs arrive and each one

September

needs to be checked closely. I wouldn't like to think of beetles or spiders being burned alive they're such useful creatures so looking them over can be a lengthy job. Then there is tidying round the back door. I always do an expert job on the parsley and the edges of my grass patch. They need a lot of pruning to keep them growing well.

It is a cat!

The worst has happened. The Dotty is here again and it has grown. The family has gone to visit somebody called Florence who lives in Italy and Florence doesn't want the Dotty. Nobody asked me if I wanted it. I should have guessed when the little wicker basket was put on the floor that something was in the air. I tried to get rid of it by chewing through the wicker but I was told off.

You should see the Dotty's tail now, it stretches for miles. Last time it was here it tried to catch it by running round in circles but couldn't reach. Now it's so long it trips over it. That's how I know it is a cat. I think long tails are very showy and common. Rabbits' scuts are so classically understated.

They haven't closed the door between our two rooms today and it has been bouncing at me again. If I stand my ground it makes itself as small as it can by flopping out but now and again it flaps a paw at me and the pins are still there. It dashed right at me under my table a few times and tried to play but I wasn't going to be pushed away from my own patch so when I'd had enough I did a very high binky, landed on top of it and gave it hard shove with my strong back legs. I was superb. It's been very polite since and stays well away from my table.

I've had a few laughs though. It tries to get into the sun hat to nap the way it did last time but it's too big now and hangs over the edges. It has no idea how silly it looks.

When it was put outside to play it used one of the garden troughs which had been nicely planted with flowers as a litter tray! It made no

September

attempt to go back inside as I always do to use the proper place. Such awful manners.

I think I'll have an early night and see what tomorrow brings. I can easily bite it if it gets too pushy. That's how my dog and I became good friends. I only had to bite her nose twice and she is much bigger than the Dotty.

More rules and regulations

A word of advice to all young rabbits. If you want to live in harmony with your humans and still be in charge there are always a few things to turn over in your mind. Rule number one is, you have to be on your toes. Once they are convinced they have you trained this is the time to confuse them. My motto is, convince and then confuse.

The word, "kisses" for instance. You will know this sound very well. Humans look on kisses as a form of affection and it's perfectly reasonable to play along. You push your face close to theirs and give them a quick lick on the nose. It pleases them and they believe they have taught you a trick. This is ok. Play along by all means. If, however, you hear "Big huggy kisses", this is a different matter altogether and the best thing to do is run. Run rabbit, run like the wind because in this house you know this is going to involve being picked up and clutched to their chests. If you are really unlucky they might sing to you while you are at your most disadvantaged and unable to breathe.

Then there's, "It's night-night-time." You probably used to give in straight away to the temptation of carrot which they wave in front of you to get you to bed. Don't be fooled. Try to ignore the carrot and think bed, a very long time on your own without attention. This is when I take to my heels and run for the nearest cover. Make sure they are chasing you round the furniture. Hide under the piano, hop behind the curtains or under a chair. Duck and dive. Pretend you are prey. Think of the good turn you are doing them. It is great exercise for everybody and they will realise you are not the pushover they thought you were.

The latest idea in my house is an attempt to teach me to sit and stay when J leaves the room for a short time to get my evening nibbles. I can do it. In fact I've done it many times with not very good grace. I had to thump hard once to remind her I was still waiting so now if I get bored and impatient I wait a minute then dash off to meet her on her way back. It speeds her up and trips her up. You see, convince and then confuse.

Finally the worst sound of all is poop-check time. Well, even they know not to make those sounds in my presence.

All you have to do is recognise a few words of their language and you can always be one step ahead. Trust me. I'm a very wise rabbit.

October

Dwarf or lop?

How could they get everything so wrong? Call themselves experienced rabbit owners? Huh! They can't even make up their minds whether I'm a mini lop or a dwarf lop. If I'm a dwarf lop is that bigger or smaller? Can I still do all the things I used to do? Will I still be the most important furry person in the house? Oh dear, I feel so insecure.

It's all to do with my weight apparently. Dwarf lops are heavier than mini lops. I'm just under 1.5 kilos which my vet says is mini lop weight. On the other hand he thinks, as a mini lop, my face should be a bit more pointed but mine is as flat as a pancake. What a terrible mix up. Am I a mongrel? I'm so confused I don't know what to do. Should I seek a second opinion do you think? Maybe try another vet practice? Can I afford it?

Oh well, I've worried enough for one day. Who cares, it's banana time. I'm only allowed the pointy end but it proves they love me whatever I look like. They don't mind if I never win a beauty contest, I'm still the most precious thing in their lives.

Raspberries

When you are small, soft, warm, cute and irresistibly cuddly like me, living indoors can be a bit of a nuisance at times. Being munched, kissed and hugged and having warm raspberries blown on the back of your neck can be inconvenient when you have already settled down for an afternoon snooze and are floating gently over a garden full of carrot tops inhaling their intoxicating perfume and mapping out where to land. Being a crepuscular animal I like to do this every afternoon for a few hours but as soon as I prepare to put down my landing gear and pucker my mouth into nibbling mode a voice cries, "There you are," and I'm disturbed again.

Of course I love the cuddles, who wouldn't but I do need a bit of privacy now and again for, well, for personal matters. Afternoons are set aside for this.

I could write a book about the private life of a rabbit if it hadn't already been

October

done. That might give them a hint about a need for my own space now and again but what if they took it to extremes and put me in a hutch at the bottom of the garden with all the slugs and snails? No, you've got to go with the flow when you live in a house with humans and have adopted them as your own. Anytime is the perfect time to put up with a few warm raspberries while I stretch out, put my chin on the floor, close my eyes and purr. This is the life.

People say the oddest things

Some neighbours called today. As a very social animal I like to welcome folk and keep up with group activities as nature intended so I dashed smartly under my table and mingled with the feet to be in the best position to catch up with village gossip.

I realised very early on humans don't give much thought beforehand to the things they say when they open their mouths. This afternoon for instance, one of them looked down at me, laughed and asked, "Which end is which?" I know I'm black all over apart from the grey tips on my front toes but people who can't tell a head from a tail shouldn't be allowed out alone. Then with no consideration for my finer feelings peered at me again and added, "I see he likes blackberries."

J was quick off the mark when she spotted my small, beautifully formed caecotroph. "Not well enough," she replied dryly. In my opinion verbalising can cause an awful lot of upset and misunderstanding.

October

My primary care giver often explains to friends who question her about life with me that my behaviour is very kittenish. She must mean my play behaviour because I am nothing like a cat, especially the Dotty. Also, when I do my speed running with my long ears flapping debonairly she says I look just like a huge black bumble bee trying to take off. You see what I mean? No consideration.

Fruit

Have you ever noticed how dangerous apples can be in autumn? They fall from the sky you know. It can be a bit of a shock if I happen to be scooting along with my head down minding my own business. Don't they know I'm a ground animal and never potter around with my head in the air waiting for fruit to fall? Why would I expect an apple to drop in unannounced? They should have more consideration for folk like me. A bang on the head with an apple could be very painful. One came pretty close to me the other day so I ran straight for home.

It's much safer in the house at apple falling time. From the back of the sofa I can stay one step ahead of things like apples while I practice mountaineering although they never seem to move while I'm watching them in the fruit bowl. Diced in a dish is the best place for them. For me, one bang on the head would be enough to remind me to stay indoors in autumn.

Other fruit is just as bad. Damsons at jam making time can be very unpredictable as well. I was quietly dozing in one of my beds recently listening to the juice slowly drip through the muslin cradle over the sink ready to make damson jelly when they completely lost their balance. They took off at the speed of light, flew through the air and splattered everything. The damson mush hit the walls, the floor and my designer boxes. It covered M who was getting jars ready and oozed its way down the sides of the cupboards.

It's no good telling people about the dangers of damsons. They will do exactly the same again at this time next year. I wonder whether they know the story of Chicken Licken who thought the sky was falling on his head when an acorn dropped down on him?

Busy again

Some days it is hard to get on with important jobs in this house. I plan my days very carefully but today as I was concentrating on getting my cardboard boxes ready for my big show, a head peeped round the door and a voice said, "Hi, Harvey, you look busy." I like it when people use my name. This time the

October

friend realised I was working and offered to help put my notice on the door. BOX EXIBITION it said. TWO CARROTS TO GET IN.

As a thank you for the help I took our visitor, Gillean, outside to show her my herbs. She has an allotment and knows about growing things. I could tell she was impressed with my small patch because she chatted to me for ages until J came out with the teapot and cups. Once they settled I wasn't needed any longer so I hopped it.

Suddenly there was an enormous commotion outside when they realised I wasn't with them in the garden. They searched under every bush and in the pond until J checked the time. "Oh, it's six- o- clock," she said. "I expect he's gone in to watch the news."

For some reason Gillean thought this was hilarious. What she found funny about watching the news at six-o-clock I can't begin to guess. I do it every day at the same time and was patiently waiting for someone to switch it on.

I'll wait until tomorrow to finish work on my boxes. I might get some peace tomorrow.

Holidays

Packing is the worst bit of a holiday. I never know what to take or what to leave behind so I end up taking everything.

My wooden stool is the most important thing because I need to sleep under something with legs. The kitchen table is far too big to fit in the car so my stool is the next best thing.

I love going to Bunny Hops because there is so much going on.

Last time I had two very nice neighbours, Jasper and Bobtail the velvet Rex rabbits who were just a few months old but quite entertaining. They were very interested in me and watched me all the time.

In the apartment on the other side were two guinea pigs, Champagne and Sparkle and they never stopped talking! You should have heard their squeaks! I couldn't understand a word they were saying. There was no reason to natter

October

all the time. If they had watched me the way Jasper and Bobtail did they might have learned how to behave in a quiet, sensible manner.

Other holiday makers didn't seem to take as much stuff as I did. I like my own things around me which probably made more work for Julie but I was happy.

While my bed was being made and my breakfast organised I hopped outside to have a look around. There were luxurious garden flats for outside rabbits so I inspected them all.

We have our own radio at Bunny Hops. A bit of background music is very relaxing. At home I often flop out and listen to opera with M, my second in command.

Now, have I forgotten anything? Chewy mat, hay bag, cuddle blankets ...

Dizzy wasps

Ventured outside today for a change but there wasn't much going on. That blackbird has started knocking figs off the tree. He thinks he owns the place and won't let any other bird near. He can't go onto the plum tree any longer because the wasps have taken it over and they are getting dizzier every day.

I don't blame the blackbird really. He has done a good job raising two families this summer because we have been over generous with my chopped grapes

October

and raisins for the babies. Birds can't carry water so chopped grapes are quite healthy. As long as I have the odd treat I don't mind sharing.

He needn't think he can move in with me in the winter. I'm not that kind hearted. He already sits on the half door and poops inward onto the porch floor to leave his messages. It's purple poop at the moment. Being a rabbit, I'm an expert on the use of poop for messages.

I'm not an expert on gardens though. Sometimes they carry me out and dangle my nose over herbs and flowers to inspire me to spend more time outside. When they put me down on the path today I counted all the way to 45 before I ran for home. That was enough fresh air for me all at once. I've managed without much of it for nine years.

November

Rabbits in the garden

These rabbits are in my friend's garden. She can watch them play through her window. I haven't met them but I'd like to. They don't have anybody telling them what not to do all day, lucky things.

I think I've worked out why it's so hard for me to clean myself properly at the rear end. They have such nicely pointed heads to help them reach in all the places a rabbit needs to reach. Mind you, there are some places I wouldn't want to find. Everybody thinks I'm adorable with my pancake-flat face.

Yesterday was a bit worrying. They shut me out by mistake and I was all by myself for what seemed like hours. I could have starved to death if I hadn't managed to stay alive by eating what was left of bean leaves, parsley, mint and rocket. Maybe outside isn't so bad after all, for a short time.

They eventually realised where I was as soon as there was nobody bobbing up and down in front of the television. That is one of the best ways I know of grabbing their attention.

Harvey van Gogh

I don't want to sound as if I'm boasting but I've decided to show my latest art work to the public. All my friends know I design cardboard boxes to order and frill armchair covers but lately I've been experimenting with other media and this is my latest wall hanging.

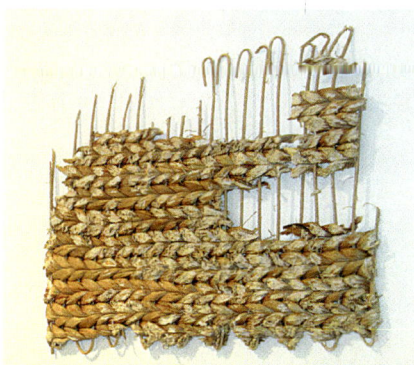

Post-Office-Margaret in our village has already asked for the next one I finish. Her special cats win silver cups so it's an honour to be recognised by somebody with such good taste.

The carpet fringe is an on-going piece of design work. It needs to be sucked and nibbled for weeks to get rid of the tightly wound fringe before I can nudge it into shape with my head. It can be a very exhausting job.

November

People insist all rabbits need a bonded partner. I don't agree. If you live with another rabbit you don't develop your originality and artistic bent. You spend time chatting to each other about rabbit stuff instead of getting on to higher things and allowing your imagination to spread in other directions. Some rabbits can be very boring.

My family is good at encouraging my talents. They give me different things to work on to keep me interested. I'm working on another chewy mat at the moment. Chill and chew I say.

Odd news

It's official. I've stopped eating carrot. Maybe not for ever but I'm putting it in my diary so I will remember such an important day. Maybe I should write to the local newspaper. "Rabbit refuses to eat carrots." It would be more interesting than some stuff they publish these days. I rip newspapers up when I find them on the floor. If you are wondering what is left to put on the shopping list there's homegrownbeanleavespeatopspointycabbageflatleafparsleymintandappleleaves and so on. When the dish is empty, I sit in it. That's known as tactics. Naturally, the family is talking about it all the time. Well, refusing carrot is very noteworthy.

"Is it his teeth do you think?"

"Open his mouth and have a look."

"No, you open his mouth, he doesn't like it."

"Should we take him to the vet?"

"Not yet. If it were his teeth he wouldn't be eating his crunchies and he is eating hay which he wouldn't do if his teeth were troubling him."

"We'll wait and see then."

Phew. No vet. I hadn't thought of that. My bedtime slice was still put down for me when the lights went out but it was too dark to see who ate it.

November

We heard from our friend Lisa to say my new hay was on its way. She has a lion head bun called Noonie to help run her Hay Experts business. The other day she couldn't find her anywhere in the house. Eventually she looked behind the sofa and Noonie had chewed a way into the back and was fast asleep inside. What a bun. It beats my frilled armchair cover! I wonder if she has her own buck rabbit. I'm free.

Strike action ahead

Going on strike can be a very tricky business for a rabbit but it looks as though it's going to be the only way to change one or two things which have spiralled out of my control. For a start the length of my grass patch needs immediate attention. Have I a great long tongue like a cow to wind round the blades and pull them up? Certainly not! I'm a nibbler. I start at one end and nibble my way to the other. Even on my back legs I couldn't reach the top. And what if there's somebody in there waiting to pounce? I've seen toads in there and spidery things.

Then there's this new performance at tea time. I'm expected to kiss J's nose before she will give me my grassy herb salad at 5-o-clock. I never had to do this in the past. It's all because she has been reading about clicker training bunnies then giving them a treat. They do this in a circus or one of those wild life parks with parrots and monkeys. M doesn't have to kiss anybody's nose before he has his tea. Why should I?

Something has to be done but what? I could refuse the salad and turn my back as we rabbits do when we want to be rude. No, not a good idea. They might take my dish away. I could give up standing in front of the vacuum cleaner as I always do to show them where to go next. I could throw all my dried grass out of my bowl. Then there's binkying in front of the television at

November

the most exciting bit of the programme and chewing furniture. It all needs to be given more thought. These things work because I've tried them all before.

I don't think I'll bother after all. What's a patch of long grass between friends and I don't hold grudges so might give it another try.

Time for tea and that kissy thing.

Breaking the rabbit habit

I am being de-conditioned, de-sensitised and maybe detoxed whatever they all mean. Hard as it is to admit, I have to face the fact I am a fringe addict. Because I have a compelling need to chew the carpet fringe every evening it has been turned under all the way round. There's not even a tiny strand left for me to pull through my teeth. Chewy mat, hay bag, willow ball and other once well loved play things are not interesting any longer to this rabbit and there's not a thing I can do about it. I'm hooked on fringes. My mind is overpowered by the idea of fringes. Any fringe will do as long as I can pick up a strand and nibble. I can go on for hours in a nibbling trance.

As long as I was quiet and not getting in the way nobody seemed interested until they noticed some of my droppings were coming out attached to a length of carpet fringe like a string of Christmas tree decorations. They know I'm an arty sort of chap so why weren't they pleased? After it happened more than once they decided to take me in hand.

Why do I do it? Am I imagining I'm in a field of juicy grass or outside by the back door trimming my pot of parsley? Who knows? Every evening I sit gloomily beside the edge of the carpet where the fringe used to be and I wait and wait.

It's all been making me have bad dreams. The last one was so awful I shot out of my bed and flew to my hidey hole stamping my foot over and over again. Maybe I was dreaming about being chased by a fox or greyhound. I've heard about these things but thought they were just fairy tales to frighten kits when they were misbehaving.

All was well though. They noticed and cuddled me on the floor until I felt better. Thank goodness I don't live in a hutch. I could have had an apoplectic attack or something even more dramatic. I like a bit of drama.

December

Managing humans

More visitors so extra work for me on the entertainment front. It can be a bit much for this aging rabbit especially the lack of respect the uninitiated can show where preferences of house buns are concerned. One of our first time visitors tried to pick me up but I saw his hands coming towards me and niftily shot through his fingers before he had a chance to haul me into the air. As you know, I never hold grudges so after a minute or two I allowed him to give me a decent sized piece of carrot to let him know he was forgiven. That's one thing he learned. Rabbits are ground creatures and hate being waved in the air like the union flag. I expect he thought my beautiful lop ears were like bird wings and was trying to get me airborne. Humans have these strange thoughts and this one was from Norway. Do they have rabbits in these foreign countries? I know there's a lot of fish there so they won't eat them.

Things are back to normal with just the three of us so I need to do a quick reminder about who is king of this bun's castle.

The dreaded myxomatosis

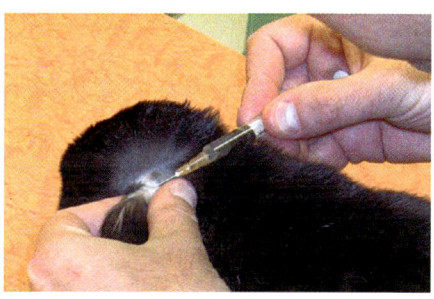

The Rabbit Welfare Association has let us know the dreaded disease is about again. Some humans don't understand the virus can be spread by a bite from a hungry flea who happens to be wandering by searching for a cosy place in somebody's fur to feast and spend the winter. How can we rabbits know when there might be one ready to jump out when we pop outside for a few minutes to snack on a few last rose petals and check the weather? Better to have the jab and be protected from myxie. It doesn't hurt a bit and I'm given a treat when we get home. I never eat it straight away of course. They have to realise I can't be blackmailed.

My vet always sends me a postcard when it is time to pay him a visit. He thinks he can fool me into thinking it will be a fun day out. I'll probably live to a ripe old age because I always do what he tells me. Well, some of the time. Well, occasionally. Well, now and again. He calls me his geriatric bun!

December

It's time to sort my space for winter evening relaxing on the sofa. I'm not allowed to scrabble though. They don't complain when I gently sort my cushions and pull the arm cover about but I'm not allowed to scrabble the seat. That's when I get a loud "NO". I can't understand their reasoning. Why can't they think like a rabbit? It works for me.

Is that a rabbit?

The day isn't going well.

Just as I was getting ready for my afternoon snooze some people came to the house to collect gifts for a raffle. They haven't been here before and they spotted me under the table.

"Oh, look, it's a rabbit!"

"Yes," agrees J. She's heard this before.

"That's unusual isn't it, a rabbit in the house? Where does it live?" IT?

"He's a house rabbit. He lives wherever he wants to."

They are country people and still don't understand so she explains again.

"He lives like a cat."

"Doesn't it run away when you open the door?"

"No, he doesn't like going out much unless we are gardening then he might if it's warm."

I think the penny is beginning to drop but they keep on digging.

"Um, doesn't it make a mess? You know, rabbits do don't they?"

J tries again. "He has a litter tray, like a cat. Sometimes there are bits about the place."

This is getting personal so I turn my back, flop out, yawn and close my eyes.

"Do you let it wander all over the house?" Still IT.

"He used to but we don't let him go upstairs since his hernia trouble. Climbing could make it worse."

"A hernia? In a rabbit? Oh, wow."

I snore loudly.

"It's snoring!!" Hey, spot on, I think to myself. They make embarrassed

December

giggles of disbelief.

"Yes," agrees J. "He does a lot of that."

They shake their heads. "A snoring house rabbit with a hernia. Well, that must be a first."

They pick up the raffle prizes and leave. I don't bother going to the door to see them off. I don't even open my eyes. I snore loudly again.

"Hush, Harve," J says waspishly. "Don't be so rude."

Me rude? That's rich!

Am I worth it?

Extra dozing mats have been put under my table now the colder weather has come. They say it makes more work because there's more to wash and keep clean. If they don't put them down I sleep on the rug and leave a few droppings lying about. I don't do it on purpose, it just sort of happens.

So now apart from these extras in the kitchen I have two litter trays, a spare bed with my teddy and cuddle blankets in the utility room, more mats there which need to be washed and bowls for my water, crunchies and greens. There are three kinds of hay in a shallow cardboard box in the sitting room and a chewy mat that drops bits. It's all my personal space.

My cuddle-cum-scrabbling towels have to be laundered regularly then I have to be brushed and clipped and cuddled all of which takes time. Why all this work for one very small rabbit? Because I'm worth it of course.

The worrying thing about all this is after being rated as a lot of trouble I'm being called a luxury. They say I cost about £700 a year to keep even without my holidays at Bunny Hops. I think that's very cheap and always try to keep costs down by not eating much hay and by sharing their human food like crispy greens and bananas. They seem to forget I don't need a hutch or a run outside so there's no cleaning and heating to deal with. When you're a thoughtful considerate chap like me you help where you can.

I put these latest grumbles down to the recession. Some buns are put out onto the street or into rescue places by families they thought loved them because they don't want the expense or trouble. I'm not going to think about that.

December

Choosing friends

As a free range house rabbit mornings tend to be the busiest time. I'm never bored doing the same thing every day. I like my ritual. First I eat my good morning scrap of carrot, carry out my ablutions, muddle my bed if somebody has straightened it, make them open all the doors so I can run through to do my daily room check then let them know when it's time for my breakfast. After this I search for the warmest spot either in front of a radiator or the place on the floor where the pipes run along. I've sorted them all.

I was living this reasonable, understated, well adjusted life until I saw some photographs of my dogs. I couldn't believe how things had changed since I lived with them. Some animals, usually dogs I have to say, allow themselves to be treated in a ridiculous fashion.

Because their feet bleed a bit if they are cut by sharp snow and ice they now have snow shoes. I sent them a message telling them exactly what I thought about dressing up dogs or any other animals for that matter. When they heard I had a very sniffy letter back.

December

"Dear Harvey," they said, "put this in your diary! You think you are the only animal who has life tagged? Do you think you are the only one who can make your family work to your rules? Well, think again rabbit. We go on holiday to other countries with the family not into Bunny Hops. We swim in rivers and in the sea to our heart's content. We go on fantastic walks, share a bedroom with our humans then come back and grab the best chairs nearest to the fire.

Do you really think you are the only one who is able to binky? Take a look at this then!

We are intrepid explorers. That's why we wear special outfits. All explorers do. Fire dogs who investigate burnt out buildings wear shoes and trained rescue dogs who search for people in collapsed buildings wear protective dog clothing. We are life saving heroes. We laugh in the face of danger. What do rabbits do? They hide in holes in the ground and under tables.

We know exactly how to wrap our humans around our paws just by gazing up at them. You still have a lot to learn Harvey so think again."

Well, really! I'm glad I don't live with them any longer.

Who needs clocks?

Weather wise it's been a mixed sort of week, warm then blowy with showers of rain. Changes in the weather put me out a bit. I can feel when there's going to be a heavy downpour with thunder. Some animals make a terrible fuss about bangs and flashes but not me. I'm a laid back sort of chap most of the time.

Talking about time, that's another speciality of mine. You might not know this but I have a magical sense telling me when things should happen. Harry Potter should have had a rabbit as a sidekick not an owl. A rabbit would have been able to feel danger looming then dash in between feet to trip up the enemy. Too late for Harry now.

Anyway, a couple of months ago for some strange and pointless reason they moved time backwards without telling me. I dashed past them at around 6 o'clock to watch the news as usual but they didn't follow. I felt such a fool when I heard the church clock strike five. Worse still they all laughed at me. I did the only possible thing at a time like that and zapped

December

into cleaning mode. Cats learned this trick from rabbits. If you think you might have done the wrong thing fudge the issue by having a good wash. Post-office-Margaret in our village says it can take her cats a month to get used to the time change. Well, cats. It would wouldn't it?

Designer homes

Place your orders please for Harvey Rabbit Cardboard Homes Incorporated, windows and doors a speciality. All shaped to your own requirement give or take a nibble or two.

If you can't put up with artistic nibbling around the house get a soft toy. A rabbit is not for you.

Rabbits have a very important reason for chewing and nibbling. If we didn't do it our teeth would grow much too long and we wouldn't be able to eat properly. Having them filed down must be horrible. I don't even like my vet poking a 'scope into my mouth.

Cats do the same sort of thing. My pen pal, half-a-tail Mimi has chewed through all the wires in her house at one time or another. An electrician often has to come and repair table lamps, computer leads and television wires because she couldn't resist a good chew. Lemon juice on wires can be a bit off-putting to a cat or a rabbit. It stopped me from nibbling a cupboard door when I was much younger.

Labrador dogs are good chewers as well. We used to have one. If rabbits hadn't invented chewing, Labradors would.

Strange happenings

I wonder what this sparkly ball is doing on my carpet. I hope they haven't brought one of those giant rabbits to live here. There wouldn't be room because most of the house space is mine. Anyway, I couldn't compete with such extraordinary sized messages especially sparkly ones. My bits are a dark hay colour and being a fastidious bun I always try to clear them up as I go along unless I decide litter tray action is needed. It's not the only thing cluttering the floor these days. Boxes I haven't seen or smelled before are

December

being wrapped in coloured paper. They must all be for me to scrabble. Paper and boxes make the best scrabbling stuff.

J has just explained it all! The packages and lights around the house are for something called Christmas. A friend brought a cardboard box filled with carrots and beetroot and parsley from their allotment. It said, "Harvey's Christmas Box." They took the beetroot leaves away because rabbits are not allowed to eat them but it all smelled wonderful, just like a deep soil burrow, a grassy field and a vegetable patch all rolled into one. I sat in it and breathed in the wonderful perfume then dived for the biggest carrot. I like this Christmas happening.

My family sat with me later and told a story to explain things. It was all about a rabbit family living together long ago in a stable full of hay. One night in the coldest part of the winter some travellers came to share the shelter and while they were there a human kitten was born. All the rabbits with their soft fur snuggled up to the baby to keep it warm and when he put his hand out to grab one of them that bunny's fur turned white. He became the Great White Rabbit who waits for us all on Rainbow Bridge.

Jingle bells

Bother! I knew there would be a snag to Christmas. I must try to remember this in future. Christmas means sprouts and jingle bells. Why won't they believe I hate sprouts? I tell them over and over again by tossing them out of my veggie dish. They sneak one in, I toss one out. They try another one. I throw it out.

Jingle bells is just as bad. All that banging on the piano hurts my ears and why do they think they can sing? I drop hint after hint by dashing into the room then sitting beside them as soon as the din starts but it never works. Have they forgotten rabbits

December

hate loud noises or don't they care? It's lucky I'm a bit deaf. My vet says lop-eared buns are more likely to be deaf because of the shape of their ear canals. We are more likely to get abscesses as well because we can't clean the canal out with a back toenail. I wouldn't like to do that anyway. Mind you, we're all a bit deaf in this house but nobody else has the excuse of being lop-eared.

There is some very good news though. We've found a home for a house rabbit somebody had put out on the street. How can people do that? How do they expect a bunny to find food on a hard pavement on its own? It now has a little girl to love it and a cosy house with food for Christmas. I am so thankful because I'm too old to bond with another rabbit. I need all the attention for myself.

I wonder what I'll find in my stocking this year? It's a very small sock so there won't be much. My first Christmas card arrived this morning. Can't see a Santa on it anywhere but it looks very cheerful.

Is this lawful?

Am I a seriously deprived rabbit? There's no hutch in the house and no large bunches of carrots hanging at nibbling height in every room. Shouldn't there be a pointy cabbage tucked under chairs in case of night starvation? Why can't I have my own television on all day long? Is the embarrassing rear end check necessary every single morning? Are these all signs of rabbit deprivation?

Even my cuddle time is getting shorter. I love my head and ears stroked and my cheeks fluffed. My friend Lennie's family has dangled some strips of gauzy material at the entrance to his den because he likes the feel of it on his face when he hops in and out. We like gentle head touches but I have nothing like that here. After just a few minutes cuddle all I hear is, "Oh, my poor back," or "Lend me a hand, I can't straighten up." I wonder whether there's a European Court of Rabbit Rights?

White stuff

My teatime is a bit miserable at the moment. Everything in the garden has turned white outside overnight. My grass and parsley and mint are buried under inches of snow. The family can't get the car up the hill and out of the village to buy my greens at the supermarket so I have to make do with odds and ends along with my dry crunchies. Unbelievably, the odd few sprout leaves still appear. They think because it's not a whole sprout I won't recognise them. I tossed my dish across the floor this morning and was told off for making a noise. I would probably starve rather than eat the smelly things.

A few sunbeams have started creeping through the window and settling on my floor so it's not all gloom and doom. Snoozing in the warm patches is the

December

best part of the day. If they happen to fall across doorways where people need to walk that's even better. There's always something a house rabbit can do to make his presence felt and show he's in charge.

Old acquaintance

This is almost the last page in my diary. Nobody has given me a new one yet for next year. Looking back I've had a very busy productive time teaching my family about house rabbits. On the whole they've been attentive and keen to follow my advice once they have understood my instructions. Reading books about us is very useful for basics but we are all different and have our own ways of doing things just like people.

I would say the three of us in this house have lots of things in common. They grow herbs in pots, I eat herbs in pots. They love reading, I enjoy turning pages of books and sorting the daily newspaper. We all like things in their proper place and share a love of bananas.

I've made loads of friends both animal and human. My Joanne who fell in love with me in a pet shop window started me on this comfortable life. M, my secondary care giver is my personal photographer and has kept a record of my life so far often catching me in embarrassing situations. My friend Celia always says where love is given it will be returned. It works well in our house.

Christmas morning

Everybody is giving other people gifts for Christmas but I didn't know what to do. I couldn't go shopping by myself and I know they don't eat hay. They don't seem to play with cardboard boxes and they never share my crunchies. I can't cut up fruit for them or put it on a plate. I had nothing to wrap in pretty paper  to put under the tree and felt very unhappy until I had a brilliant idea. I could leave them something extra special on Christmas morning. Something I know they really like because they always wrap it up and take it away with them to keep. I left two pieces of my very own poo on the kitchen floor instead of in the utility room! It was the first thing they saw when they came downstairs and the smile on their faces told me I had made the right choice.

"Thank you Harve," they said, then gave me a big Christmas kiss.

Everyone should have bit of Heaven in
their lives and you are ours Harvey.